# Fantasy Landscapes
## Mosaic Color By Numbers
## Coloring Book For Adults

A MAGICAL EXTREME ADULT COLOR-BY-NUMBER BOOK OF DETAILED HIDDEN NATURE, SECRET GARDENS, AND FAIRYTALE CITIES

BY COLOR QUESTOPIA

Copyright © 2020

All rights reserved. No part of this publication may be reproduced, distributed, or transmitted in any form or by any means, including photocopying, recording, or other electronic or mechanical methods, without the prior written permission of the publisher

# Color By Number Tips

1. **Relax and have fun**

   Let your cares slip away as you color the images. Take your time. Coloring is a meditative activity and there's no wrong way to do it. Feel free to color as you listen to music, watch TV, lounge in bed- do whatever relaxes you most! You can also color while you're out and about- on the train or at a cafe- take the book with you anywhere you go. Coloring is therapeutic and is great for stress relief and relaxation!

2. **Colors corresponding to each number are shown on the back cover of the book - THIS BOOK HAS OUR NEW COLORING SYSTEM WHERE EVERY COLOR IN EVERY BOOK IS SHOWN ON THE BACK OF THE BOOK**

   Each number corresponds to a color shown on the back of the book. Because this is our new system, there may be colors and numbers on the back that aren't in this book- that's totally okay. Just follow the numbers on the images in this book, and match those numbers to colors. You can match the color as closely as you like- but feel free to change the color or the shade if you don't have the exact color match- that's totally fine. Although this is a color by number book, it's completely okay to get creative and color the images with whichever colors you like and have. The numbers are there to be a guide and to allow you to color without having to focus your energy on choosing colors.

3. **Choose your coloring tools**

   Everyone has their favorite coloring markers, crayons, pencils, pens- even paints! Feel free to color with any tool that you like! If you choose markers or paints, we recommend putting a blank sheet of paper or cardboard behind each image, so that your colors don't run onto the next image.

1. Black
2. Golden
3. Light Red
4. Medium Red
5. Red
6. Dark Red
7. Lemon Yellow
8. Light Yellow
9. Yellow
10. Dark Yellow
11. Bright Orange
12. Light Orange
13. Medium Orange
14. Orange
15. Dark Orange
16. Chocolate
17. Light Brown
18. Medium Brown
19. Brown
20. Dark Brown
21. Neon Green
22. Light Green
23. Medium Green
24. Green
25. Army Green
26. Dark Green
27. Peach
28. Light Pink
29. Medium Pink
30. Pink
31. Hot Pink
32. Dark Pink
33. Medium Purple
34. Purple
35. Light Violet
36. Soft Violet
37. Violet
38. Dark Violet
39. Baby Blue
40. Sky Blue
41. Light Blue
42. Medium Blue
43. Blue
44. Dark Blue
45. Navy Blue
46. Beige
47. Light Gray
48. Medium Gray
49. Gray
50. Dark Gray

1. Black
2. Golden
3. Light Red
4. Medium Red
5. Red
6. Dark Red
7. Lemon Yellow
8. Light Yellow
9. Yellow
10. Dark Yellow
11. Bright Orange
12. Light Orange
13. Medium Orange
14. Orange
15. Dark Orange
16. Chocolate
17. Light Brown
18. Medium Brown
19. Brown
20. Dark Brown
21. Neon Green
22. Light Green
23. Medium Green
24. Green
25. Army Green
26. Dark Green
27. Peach
28. Light Pink
29. Medium Pink
30. Pink
31. Hot Pink
32. Dark Pink
33. Medium Purple
34. Purple
35. Light Violet
36. Soft Violet
37. Violet
38. Dark Violet
39. Baby Blue
40. Sky Blue
41. Light Blue
42. Medium Blue
43. Blue
44. Dark Blue
45. Navy Blue
46. Beige
47. Light Gray
48. Medium Gray
49. Gray
50. Dark Gray

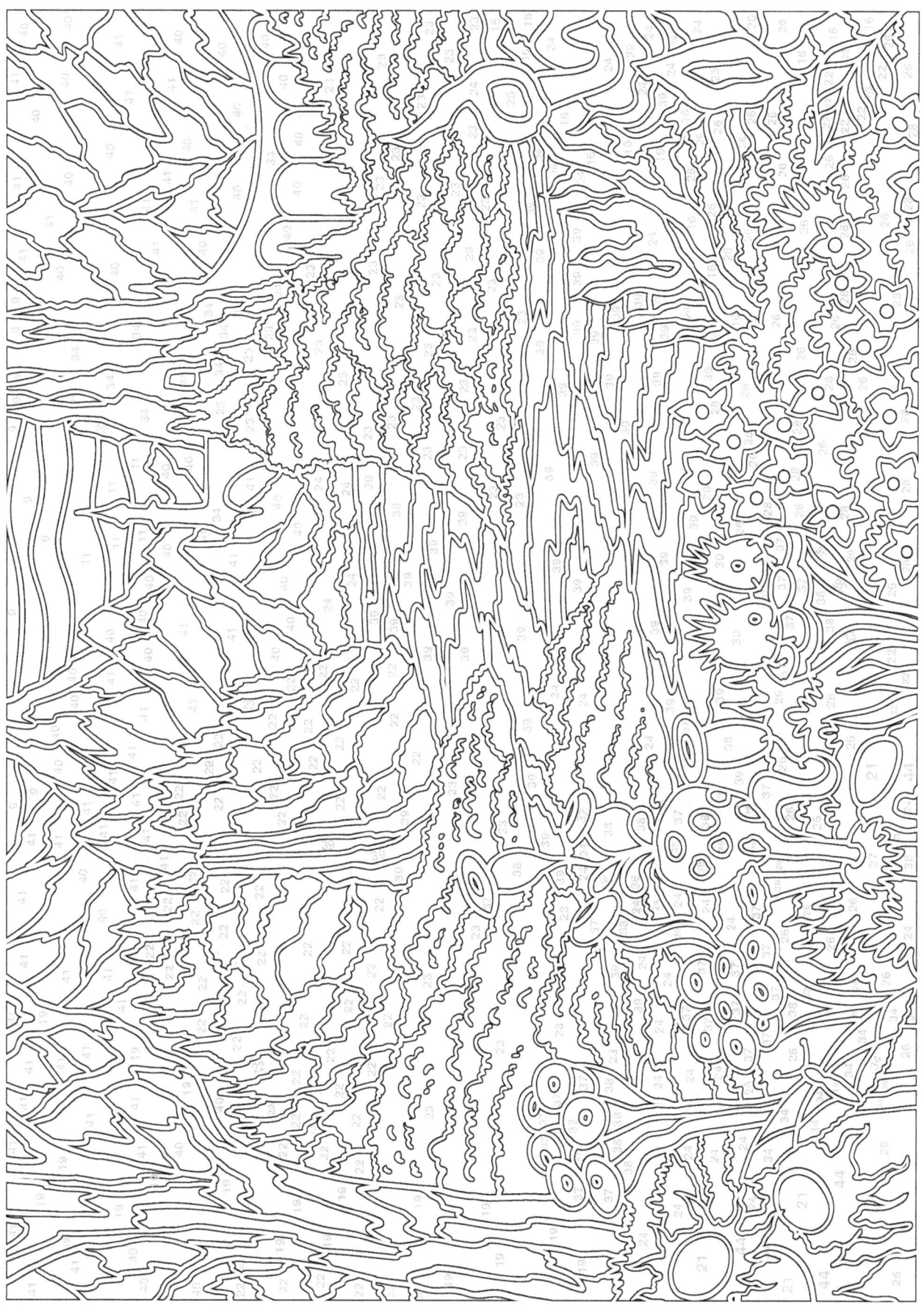

1. Black
2. Golden
3. Light Red
4. Medium Red
5. Red
6. Dark Red
7. Lemon Yellow
8. Light Yellow
9. Yellow
10. Dark Yellow
11. Bright Orange
12. Light Orange
13. Medium Orange
14. Orange
15. Dark Orange
16. Chocolate
17. Light Brown
18. Medium Brown
19. Brown
20. Dark Brown
21. Neon Green
22. Light Green
23. Medium Green
24. Green
25. Army Green
26. Dark Green
27. Peach
28. Light Pink
29. Medium Pink
30. Pink
31. Hot Pink
32. Dark Pink
33. Medium Purple
34. Purple
35. Light Violet
36. Soft Violet
37. Violet
38. Dark Violet
39. Baby Blue
40. Sky Blue
41. Light Blue
42. Medium Blue
43. Blue
44. Dark Blue
45. Navy Blue
46. Beige
47. Light Gray
48. Medium Gray
49. Gray
50. Dark Gray

1. Black
2. Golden
3. Light Red
4. Medium Red
5. Red
6. Dark Red
7. Lemon Yellow
8. Light Yellow
9. Yellow
10. Dark Yellow
11. Bright Orange
12. Light Orange
13. Medium Orange
14. Orange
15. Dark Orange
16. Chocolate
17. Light Brown
18. Medium Brown
19. Brown
20. Dark Brown
21. Neon Green
22. Light Green
23. Medium Green
24. Green
25. Army Green
26. Dark Green
27. Peach
28. Light Pink
29. Medium Pink
30. Pink
31. Hot Pink
32. Dark Pink
33. Medium Purple
34. Purple
35. Light Violet
36. Soft Violet
37. Violet
38. Dark Violet
39. Baby Blue
40. Sky Blue
41. Light Blue
42. Medium Blue
43. Blue
44. Dark Blue
45. Navy Blue
46. Beige
47. Light Gray
48. Medium Gray
49. Gray
50. Dark Gray

1. Black
2. Golden
3. Light Red
4. Medium Red
5. Red
6. Dark Red
7. Lemon Yellow
8. Light Yellow
9. Yellow
10. Dark Yellow
11. Bright Orange
12. Light Orange
13. Medium Orange
14. Orange
15. Dark Orange
16. Chocolate
17. Light Brown
18. Medium Brown
19. Brown
20. Dark Brown
21. Neon Green
22. Light Green
23. Medium Green
24. Green
25. Army Green
26. Dark Green
27. Peach
28. Light Pink
29. Medium Pink
30. Pink
31. Hot Pink
32. Dark Pink
33. Medium Purple
34. Purple
35. Light Violet
36. Soft Violet
37. Violet
38. Dark Violet
39. Baby Blue
40. Sky Blue
41. Light Blue
42. Medium Blue
43. Blue
44. Dark Blue
45. Navy Blue
46. Beige
47. Light Gray
48. Medium Gray
49. Gray
50. Dark Gray

1. Black
2. Golden
3. Light Red
4. Medium Red
5. Red
6. Dark Red
7. Lemon Yellow
8. Light Yellow
9. Yellow
10. Dark Yellow
11. Bright Orange
12. Light Orange
13. Medium Orange
14. Orange
15. Dark Orange
16. Chocolate
17. Light Brown
18. Medium Brown
19. Brown
20. Dark Brown
21. Neon Green
22. Light Green
23. Medium Green
24. Green
25. Army Green
26. Dark Green
27. Peach
28. Light Pink
29. Medium Pink
30. Pink
31. Hot Pink
32. Dark Pink
33. Medium Purple
34. Purple
35. Light Violet
36. Soft Violet
37. Violet
38. Dark Violet
39. Baby Blue
40. Sky Blue
41. Light Blue
42. Medium Blue
43. Blue
44. Dark Blue
45. Navy Blue
46. Beige
47. Light Gray
48. Medium Gray
49. Gray
50. Dark Gray

1. Black
2. Golden
3. Light Red
4. Medium Red
5. Red
6. Dark Red
7. Lemon Yellow
8. Light Yellow
9. Yellow
10. Dark Yellow
11. Bright Orange
12. Light Orange
13. Medium Orange
14. Orange
15. Dark Orange
16. Chocolate
17. Light Brown
18. Medium Brown
19. Brown
20. Dark Brown
21. Neon Green
22. Light Green
23. Medium Green
24. Green
25. Army Green
26. Dark Green
27. Peach
28. Light Pink
29. Medium Pink
30. Pink
31. Hot Pink
32. Dark Pink
33. Medium Purple
34. Purple
35. Light Violet
36. Soft Violet
37. Violet
38. Dark Violet
39. Baby Blue
40. Sky Blue
41. Light Blue
42. Medium Blue
43. Blue
44. Dark Blue
45. Navy Blue
46. Beige
47. Light Gray
48. Medium Gray
49. Gray
50. Dark Gray

1. Black
2. Golden
3. Light Red
4. Medium Red
5. Red
6. Dark Red
7. Lemon Yellow
8. Light Yellow
9. Yellow
10. Dark Yellow
11. Bright Orange
12. Light Orange
13. Medium Orange
14. Orange
15. Dark Orange
16. Chocolate
17. Light Brown
18. Medium Brown
19. Brown
20. Dark Brown
21. Neon Green
22. Light Green
23. Medium Green
24. Green
25. Army Green
26. Dark Green
27. Peach
28. Light Pink
29. Medium Pink
30. Pink
31. Hot Pink
32. Dark Pink
33. Medium Purple
34. Purple
35. Light Violet
36. Soft Violet
37. Violet
38. Dark Violet
39. Baby Blue
40. Sky Blue
41. Light Blue
42. Medium Blue
43. Blue
44. Dark Blue
45. Navy Blue
46. Beige
47. Light Gray
48. Medium Gray
49. Gray
50. Dark Gray

1. Black
2. Golden
3. Light Red
4. Medium Red
5. Red
6. Dark Red
7. Lemon Yellow
8. Light Yellow
9. Yellow
10. Dark Yellow
11. Bright Orange
12. Light Orange
13. Medium Orange
14. Orange
15. Dark Orange
16. Chocolate
17. Light Brown
18. Medium Brown
19. Brown
20. Dark Brown
21. Neon Green
22. Light Green
23. Medium Green
24. Green
25. Army Green
26. Dark Green
27. Peach
28. Light Pink
29. Medium Pink
30. Pink
31. Hot Pink
32. Dark Pink
33. Medium Purple
34. Purple
35. Light Violet
36. Soft Violet
37. Violet
38. Dark Violet
39. Baby Blue
40. Sky Blue
41. Light Blue
42. Medium Blue
43. Blue
44. Dark Blue
45. Navy Blue
46. Beige
47. Light Gray
48. Medium Gray
49. Gray
50. Dark Gray

1. Black
2. Golden
3. Light Red
4. Medium Red
5. Red
6. Dark Red
7. Lemon Yellow
8. Light Yellow
9. Yellow
10. Dark Yellow
11. Bright Orange
12. Light Orange
13. Medium Orange
14. Orange
15. Dark Orange
16. Chocolate
17. Light Brown
18. Medium Brown
19. Brown
20. Dark Brown
21. Neon Green
22. Light Green
23. Medium Green
24. Green
25. Army Green
26. Dark Green
27. Peach
28. Light Pink
29. Medium Pink
30. Pink
31. Hot Pink
32. Dark Pink
33. Medium Purple
34. Purple
35. Light Violet
36. Soft Violet
37. Violet
38. Dark Violet
39. Baby Blue
40. Sky Blue
41. Light Blue
42. Medium Blue
43. Blue
44. Dark Blue
45. Navy Blue
46. Beige
47. Light Gray
48. Medium Gray
49. Gray
50. Dark Gray

1. Black
2. Golden
3. Light Red
4. Medium Red
5. Red
6. Dark Red
7. Lemon Yellow
8. Light Yellow
9. Yellow
10. Dark Yellow
11. Bright Orange
12. Light Orange
13. Medium Orange
14. Orange
15. Dark Orange
16. Chocolate
17. Light Brown
18. Medium Brown
19. Brown
20. Dark Brown
21. Neon Green
22. Light Green
23. Medium Green
24. Green
25. Army Green
26. Dark Green
27. Peach
28. Light Pink
29. Medium Pink
30. Pink
31. Hot Pink
32. Dark Pink
33. Medium Purple
34. Purple
35. Light Violet
36. Soft Violet
37. Violet
38. Dark Violet
39. Baby Blue
40. Sky Blue
41. Light Blue
42. Medium Blue
43. Blue
44. Dark Blue
45. Navy Blue
46. Beige
47. Light Gray
48. Medium Gray
49. Gray
50. Dark Gray

1. Black
2. Golden
3. Light Red
4. Medium Red
5. Red
6. Dark Red
7. Lemon Yellow
8. Light Yellow
9. Yellow
10. Dark Yellow
11. Bright Orange
12. Light Orange
13. Medium Orange
14. Orange
15. Dark Orange
16. Chocolate
17. Light Brown
18. Medium Brown
19. Brown
20. Dark Brown
21. Neon Green
22. Light Green
23. Medium Green
24. Green
25. Army Green
26. Dark Green
27. Peach
28. Light Pink
29. Medium Pink
30. Pink
31. Hot Pink
32. Dark Pink
33. Medium Purple
34. Purple
35. Light Violet
36. Soft Violet
37. Violet
38. Dark Violet
39. Baby Blue
40. Sky Blue
41. Light Blue
42. Medium Blue
43. Blue
44. Dark Blue
45. Navy Blue
46. Beige
47. Light Gray
48. Medium Gray
49. Gray
50. Dark Gray

1. Black
2. Golden
3. Light Red
4. Medium Red
5. Red
6. Dark Red
7. Lemon Yellow
8. Light Yellow
9. Yellow
10. Dark Yellow
11. Bright Orange
12. Light Orange
13. Medium Orange
14. Orange
15. Dark Orange
16. Chocolate
17. Light Brown
18. Medium Brown
19. Brown
20. Dark Brown
21. Neon Green
22. Light Green
23. Medium Green
24. Green
25. Army Green
26. Dark Green
27. Peach
28. Light Pink
29. Medium Pink
30. Pink
31. Hot Pink
32. Dark Pink
33. Medium Purple
34. Purple
35. Light Violet
36. Soft Violet
37. Violet
38. Dark Violet
39. Baby Blue
40. Sky Blue
41. Light Blue
42. Medium Blue
43. Blue
44. Dark Blue
45. Navy Blue
46. Beige
47. Light Gray
48. Medium Gray
49. Gray
50. Dark Gray

1. Black
2. Golden
3. Light Red
4. Medium Red
5. Red
6. Dark Red
7. Lemon Yellow
8. Light Yellow
9. Yellow
10. Dark Yellow
11. Bright Orange
12. Light Orange
13. Medium Orange
14. Orange
15. Dark Orange
16. Chocolate
17. Light Brown
18. Medium Brown
19. Brown
20. Dark Brown
21. Neon Green
22. Light Green
23. Medium Green
24. Green
25. Army Green
26. Dark Green
27. Peach
28. Light Pink
29. Medium Pink
30. Pink
31. Hot Pink
32. Dark Pink
33. Medium Purple
34. Purple
35. Light Violet
36. Soft Violet
37. Violet
38. Dark Violet
39. Baby Blue
40. Sky Blue
41. Light Blue
42. Medium Blue
43. Blue
44. Dark Blue
45. Navy Blue
46. Beige
47. Light Gray
48. Medium Gray
49. Gray
50. Dark Gray

1. Black
2. Golden
3. Light Red
4. Medium Red
5. Red
6. Dark Red
7. Lemon Yellow
8. Light Yellow
9. Yellow
10. Dark Yellow
11. Bright Orange
12. Light Orange
13. Medium Orange
14. Orange
15. Dark Orange
16. Chocolate
17. Light Brown
18. Medium Brown
19. Brown
20. Dark Brown
21. Neon Green
22. Light Green
23. Medium Green
24. Green
25. Army Green
26. Dark Green
27. Peach
28. Light Pink
29. Medium Pink
30. Pink
31. Hot Pink
32. Dark Pink
33. Medium Purple
34. Purple
35. Light Violet
36. Soft Violet
37. Violet
38. Dark Violet
39. Baby Blue
40. Sky Blue
41. Light Blue
42. Medium Blue
43. Blue
44. Dark Blue
45. Navy Blue
46. Beige
47. Light Gray
48. Medium Gray
49. Gray
50. Dark Gray

1. Black
2. Golden
3. Light Red
4. Medium Red
5. Red
6. Dark Red
7. Lemon Yellow
8. Light Yellow
9. Yellow
10. Dark Yellow
11. Bright Orange
12. Light Orange
13. Medium Orange
14. Orange
15. Dark Orange
16. Chocolate
17. Light Brown
18. Medium Brown
19. Brown
20. Dark Brown
21. Neon Green
22. Light Green
23. Medium Green
24. Green
25. Army Green
26. Dark Green
27. Peach
28. Light Pink
29. Medium Pink
30. Pink
31. Hot Pink
32. Dark Pink
33. Medium Purple
34. Purple
35. Light Violet
36. Soft Violet
37. Violet
38. Dark Violet
39. Baby Blue
40. Sky Blue
41. Light Blue
42. Medium Blue
43. Blue
44. Dark Blue
45. Navy Blue
46. Beige
47. Light Gray
48. Medium Gray
49. Gray
50. Dark Gray

1. Black
2. Golden
3. Light Red
4. Medium Red
5. Red
6. Dark Red
7. Lemon Yellow
8. Light Yellow
9. Yellow
10. Dark Yellow
11. Bright Orange
12. Light Orange
13. Medium Orange
14. Orange
15. Dark Orange
16. Chocolate
17. Light Brown
18. Medium Brown
19. Brown
20. Dark Brown
21. Neon Green
22. Light Green
23. Medium Green
24. Green
25. Army Green
26. Dark Green
27. Peach
28. Light Pink
29. Medium Pink
30. Pink
31. Hot Pink
32. Dark Pink
33. Medium Purple
34. Purple
35. Light Violet
36. Soft Violet
37. Violet
38. Dark Violet
39. Baby Blue
40. Sky Blue
41. Light Blue
42. Medium Blue
43. Blue
44. Dark Blue
45. Navy Blue
46. Beige
47. Light Gray
48. Medium Gray
49. Gray
50. Dark Gray

1. Black
2. Golden
3. Light Red
4. Medium Red
5. Red
6. Dark Red
7. Lemon Yellow
8. Light Yellow
9. Yellow
10. Dark Yellow
11. Bright Orange
12. Light Orange
13. Medium Orange
14. Orange
15. Dark Orange
16. Chocolate
17. Light Brown
18. Medium Brown
19. Brown
20. Dark Brown
21. Neon Green
22. Light Green
23. Medium Green
24. Green
25. Army Green
26. Dark Green
27. Peach
28. Light Pink
29. Medium Pink
30. Pink
31. Hot Pink
32. Dark Pink
33. Medium Purple
34. Purple
35. Light Violet
36. Soft Violet
37. Violet
38. Dark Violet
39. Baby Blue
40. Sky Blue
41. Light Blue
42. Medium Blue
43. Blue
44. Dark Blue
45. Navy Blue
46. Beige
47. Light Gray
48. Medium Gray
49. Gray
50. Dark Gray

1. Black
2. Golden
3. Light Red
4. Medium Red
5. Red
6. Dark Red
7. Lemon Yellow
8. Light Yellow
9. Yellow
10. Dark Yellow
11. Bright Orange
12. Light Orange
13. Medium Orange
14. Orange
15. Dark Orange
16. Chocolate
17. Light Brown
18. Medium Brown
19. Brown
20. Dark Brown
21. Neon Green
22. Light Green
23. Medium Green
24. Green
25. Army Green
26. Dark Green
27. Peach
28. Light Pink
29. Medium Pink
30. Pink
31. Hot Pink
32. Dark Pink
33. Medium Purple
34. Purple
35. Light Violet
36. Soft Violet
37. Violet
38. Dark Violet
39. Baby Blue
40. Sky Blue
41. Light Blue
42. Medium Blue
43. Blue
44. Dark Blue
45. Navy Blue
46. Beige
47. Light Gray
48. Medium Gray
49. Gray
50. Dark Gray

1. Black
2. Golden
3. Light Red
4. Medium Red
5. Red
6. Dark Red
7. Lemon Yellow
8. Light Yellow
9. Yellow
10. Dark Yellow
11. Bright Orange
12. Light Orange
13. Medium Orange
14. Orange
15. Dark Orange
16. Chocolate
17. Light Brown
18. Medium Brown
19. Brown
20. Dark Brown
21. Neon Green
22. Light Green
23. Medium Green
24. Green
25. Army Green
26. Dark Green
27. Peach
28. Light Pink
29. Medium Pink
30. Pink
31. Hot Pink
32. Dark Pink
33. Medium Purple
34. Purple
35. Light Violet
36. Soft Violet
37. Violet
38. Dark Violet
39. Baby Blue
40. Sky Blue
41. Light Blue
42. Medium Blue
43. Blue
44. Dark Blue
45. Navy Blue
46. Beige
47. Light Gray
48. Medium Gray
49. Gray
50. Dark Gray

ENJOY BONUS IMAGES FROM SOME OF OUR OTHER FUN COLOR BY NUMBER BOOKS!

FIND ALL OF OUR BOOKS ON AMAZON

# Autumn
## Mosaic Adult Color By Numbers Magical Fall Coloring Book

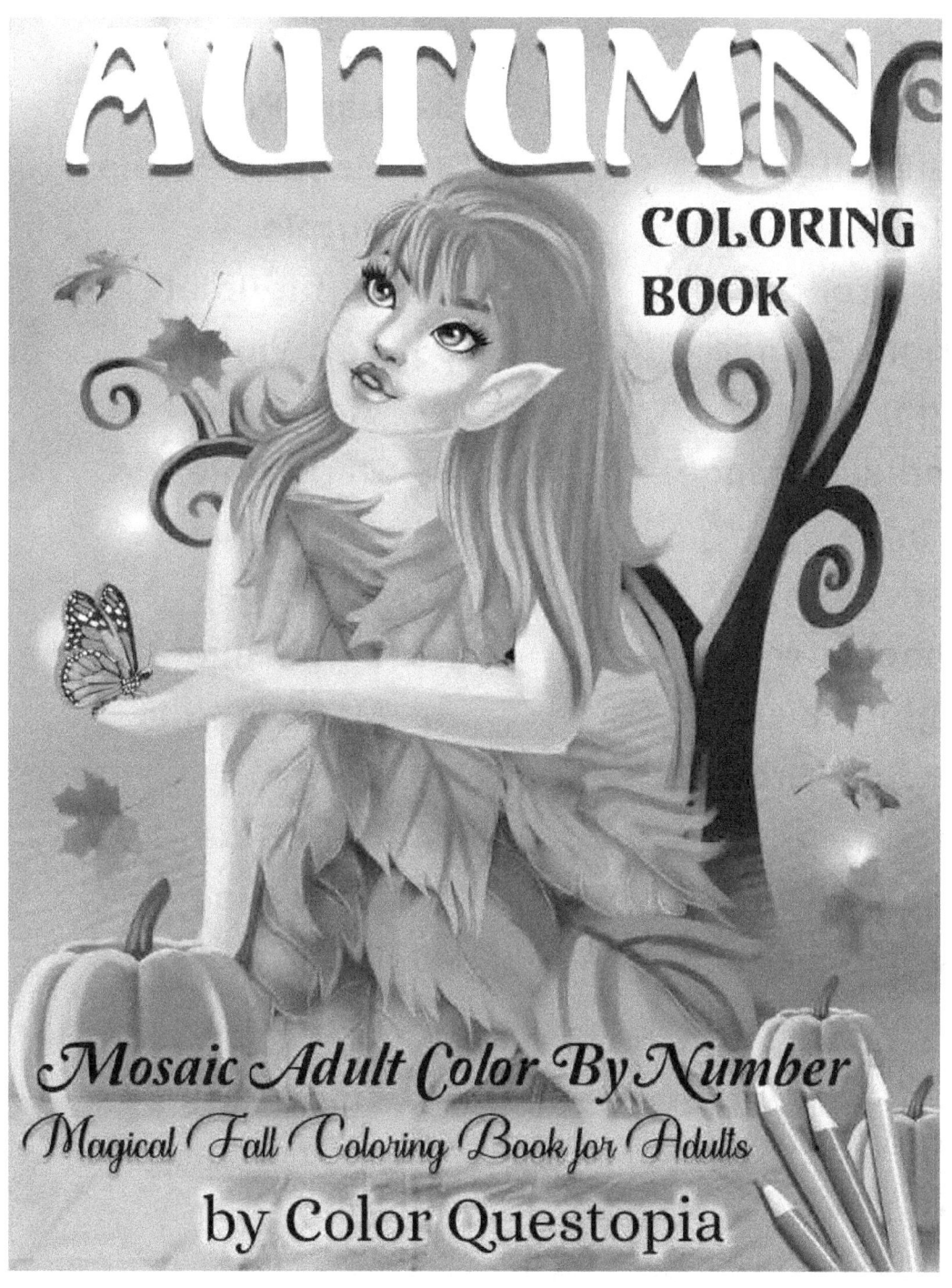

1. Black
2. Golden
3. Light Red
4. Medium Red
5. Red
6. Dark Red
7. Lemon Yellow
8. Light Yellow
9. Yellow
10. Dark Yellow
11. Bright Orange
12. Light Orange
13. Medium Orange
14. Orange
15. Dark Orange
16. Chocolate
17. Light Brown
18. Medium Brown
19. Brown
20. Dark Brown
21. Neon Green
22. Light Green
23. Medium Green
24. Green
25. Army Green
26. Dark Green
27. Peach
28. Light Pink
29. Medium Pink
30. Pink
31. Hot Pink
32. Dark Pink
33. Medium Purple
34. Purple
35. Light Violet
36. Soft Violet
37. Violet
38. Dark Violet
39. Baby Blue
40. Sky Blue
41. Light Blue
42. Medium Blue
43. Blue
44. Dark Blue
45. Navy Blue
46. Beige
47. Light Gray
48. Medium Gray
49. Gray
50. Dark Gray

# National Parks
## Mosaic Color By Number Coloring Book For Adults

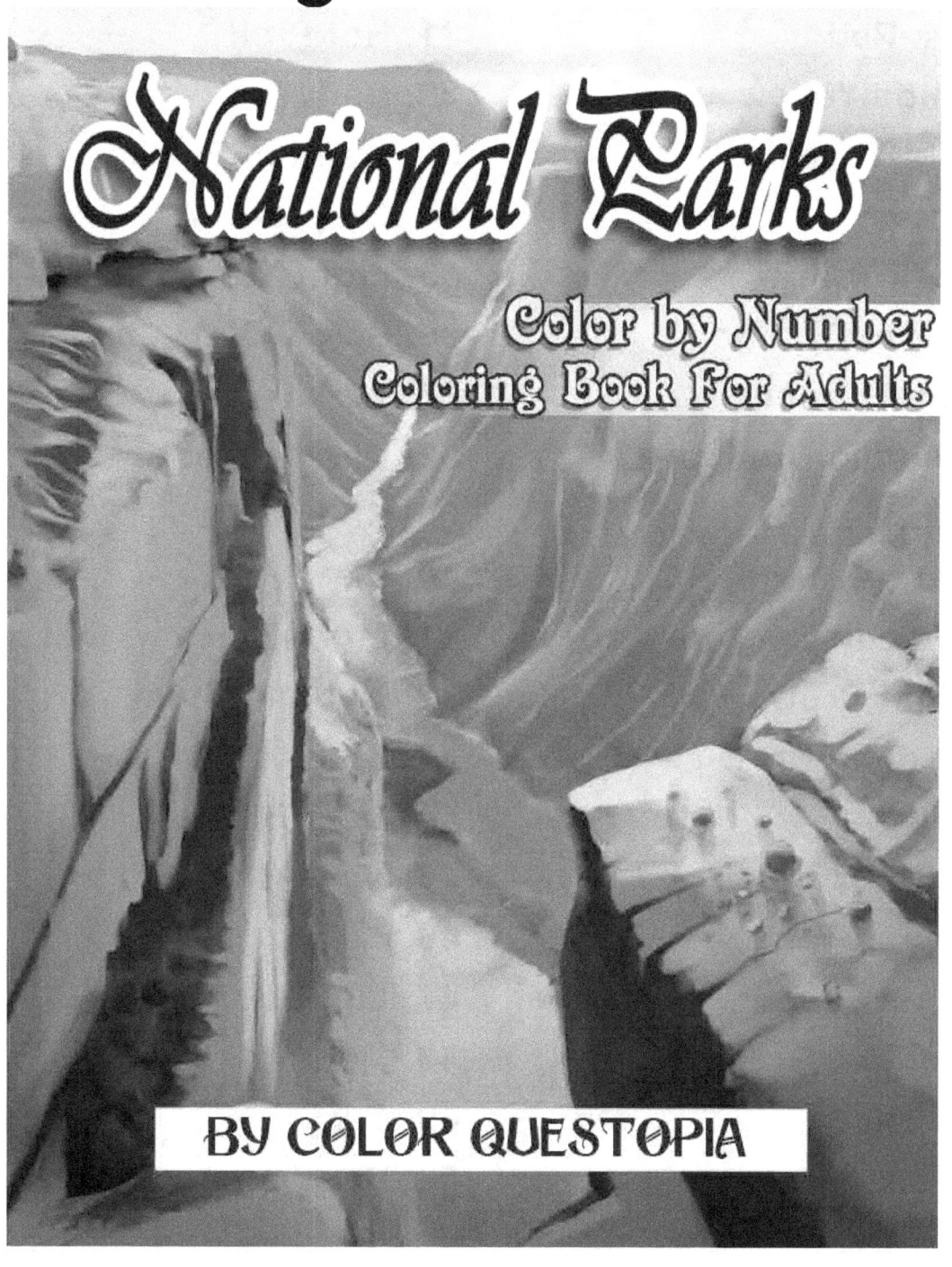

1. Black
2. Golden
3. Light Red
4. Medium Red
5. Red
6. Dark Red
7. Lemon Yellow
8. Light Yellow
9. Yellow
10. Dark Yellow
11. Bright Orange
12. Light Orange
13. Medium Orange
14. Orange
15. Dark Orange
16. Chocolate
17. Light Brown
18. Medium Brown
19. Brown
20. Dark Brown
21. Neon Green
22. Light Green
23. Medium Green
24. Green
25. Army Green
26. Dark Green
27. Peach
28. Light Pink
29. Medium Pink
30. Pink
31. Hot Pink
32. Dark Pink
33. Medium Purple
34. Purple
35. Light Violet
36. Soft Violet
37. Violet
38. Dark Violet
39. Baby Blue
40. Sky Blue
41. Light Blue
42. Medium Blue
43. Blue
44. Dark Blue
45. Navy Blue
46. Beige
47. Light Gray
48. Medium Gray
49. Gray
50. Dark Gray

Acadia National Park - Maine

# Camping
## Color By Numbers
## Coloring Book

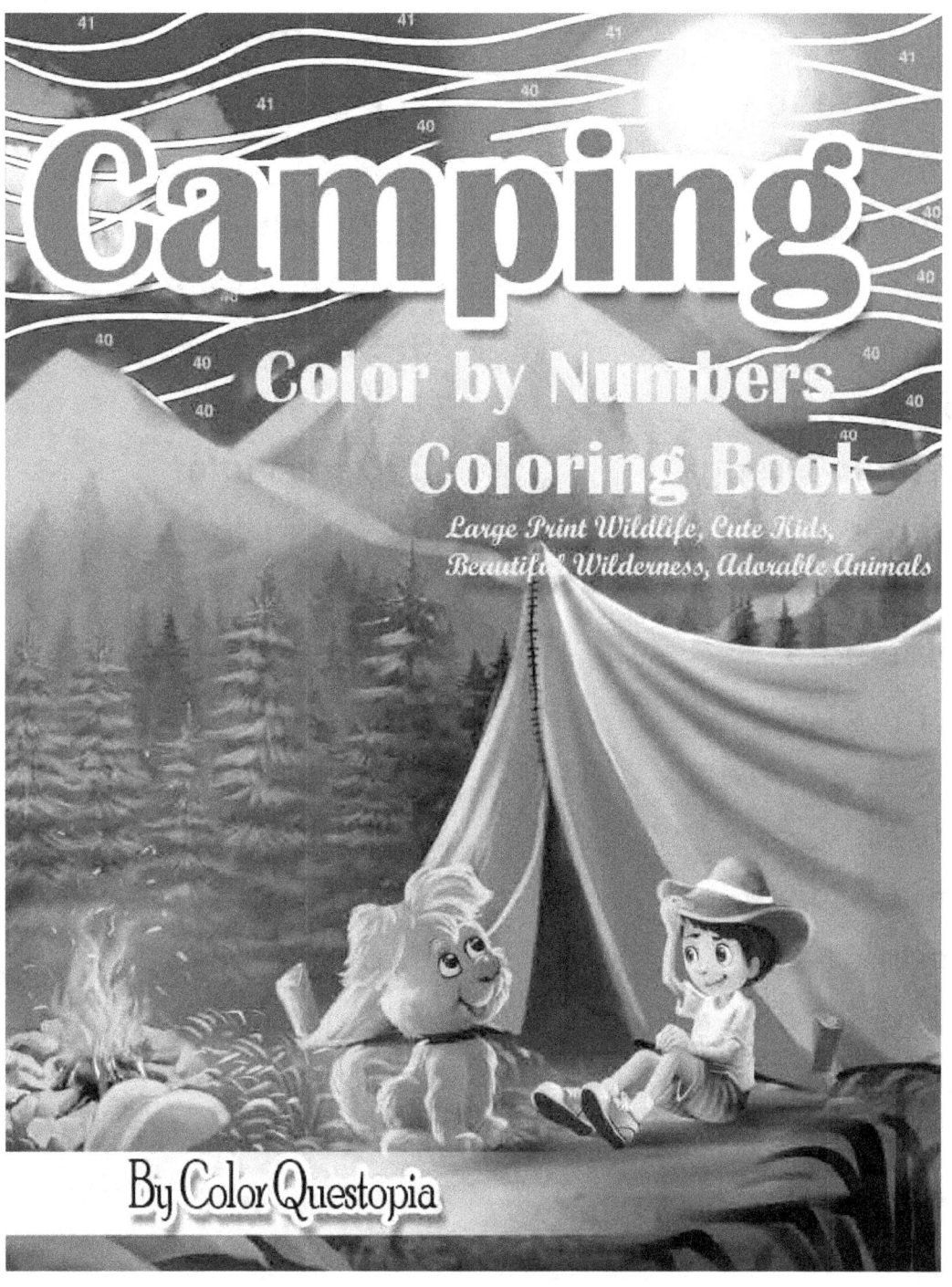

1. Black
2. Golden
3. Light Red
4. Medium Red
5. Red
6. Dark Red
7. Lemon Yellow
8. Light Yellow
9. Yellow
10. Dark Yellow
11. Bright Orange
12. Light Orange
13. Medium Orange
14. Orange
15. Dark Orange
16. Chocolate
17. Light Brown
18. Medium Brown
19. Brown
20. Dark Brown
21. Neon Green
22. Light Green
23. Medium Green
24. Green
25. Army Green
26. Dark Green
27. Peach
28. Light Pink
29. Medium Pink
30. Pink
31. Hot Pink
32. Dark Pink
33. Medium Purple
34. Purple
35. Light Violet
36. Soft Violet
37. Violet
38. Dark Violet
39. Baby Blue
40. Sky Blue
41. Light Blue
42. Medium Blue
43. Blue
44. Dark Blue
45. Navy Blue
46. Beige
47. Light Gray
48. Medium Gray
49. Gray
50. Dark Gray

# Princess Coloring Book
## Large Print Mosaic
## Color By Number

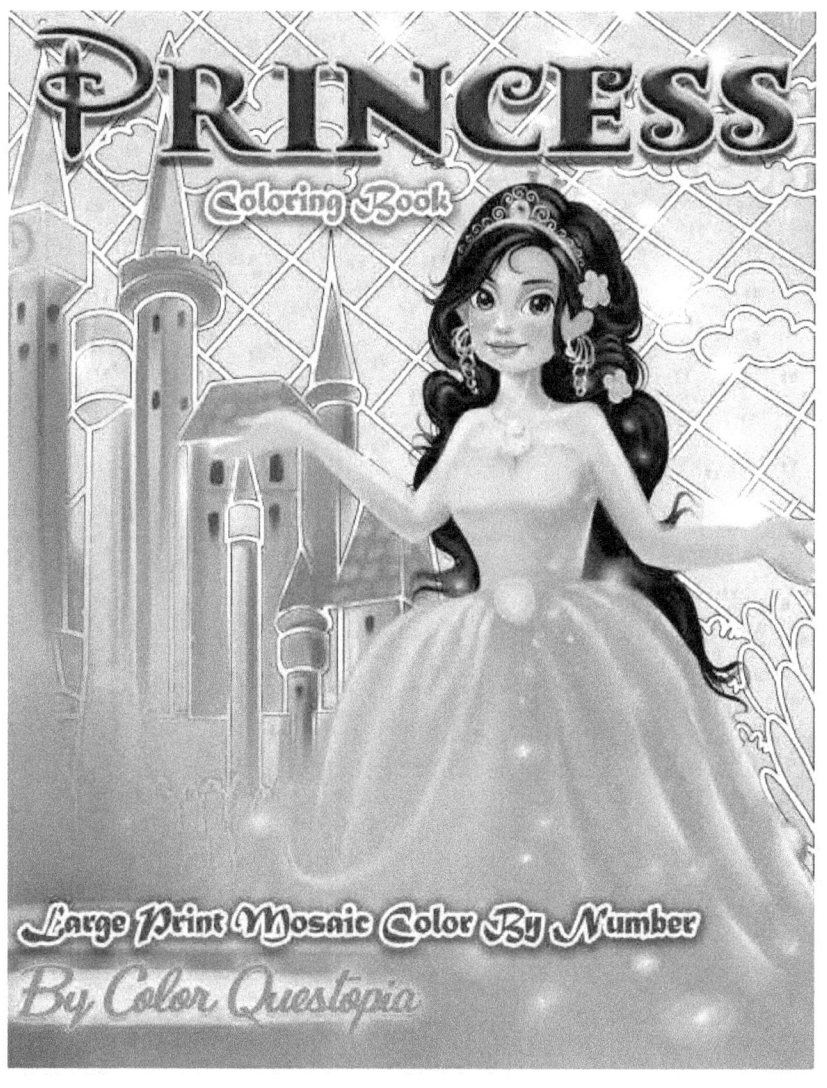

1. Black
2. White
3. Peach
4. Light Brown
5. Pink
6. Dark Pink
7. Yellow
8. Green
9. Baby Blue
10. Light Pink
11. Blue
12. Orange
13. Light Orange
14. Red
15. Violet

Beautiful Cities and Landmarks
Color by Number
Mosaic World Geography
Coloring Book For Adults

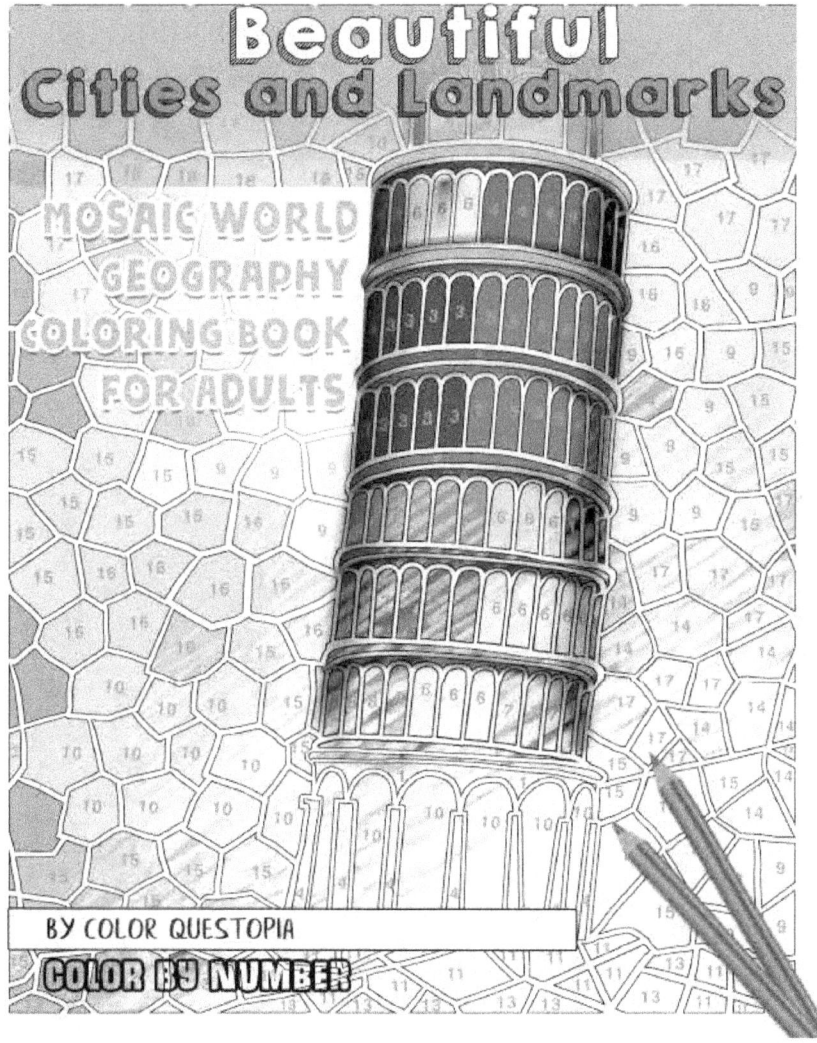

1. Light Brown
2. Medium Brown
3. Dark Brown
4. Gray
5. Dark Gray
6. Yellow
7. Orange
8. Brown
9. Soft Violet
10. Green
11. Deep Green
12. Light Green
13. Medium Gray
14. Light Gray
15. Navy Blue
16. Sky Blue
17. Light Pink
18. Dark Yellow

www.ingramcontent.com/pod-product-compliance
Lightning Source LLC
Chambersburg PA
CBHW081458220526
45466CB00008B/2699